Cricket

Written in association with the
England and Wales Cricket Board

ECB

Published in 2009 by

A & C Black Publishers Ltd
36 Soho Square, London W1D 3QY
www.acblack.com

Fifth edition 2009

ISBN: 978 07136 8374 5

Note: Whilst every effort has been made to ensure
that the content of this book is as technically accurate
and as sound as possible, neither the authors nor the
publishers can accept responsibility for any injury or
loss sustained as a result of the use of this material.

This book is produced using paper that is made
from wood grown in managed, sustainable forests.
It is natural, renewable and recyclable. The logging
and manufacturing processes conform to the
environmental regulations of the country of origin.

Acknowledgements
Cover and inside design by James Winrow and
Tom Morris.
Cover photograph of Kevin Pietersen courtesy
of PA Photos.
We would like to thank the following for permission
to reproduce photos: ECB pages 6, 22, 24, 33, 37,
39, 46, 57; iStockphoto pages 5, 7, 55; PA Photos
pages 4, 10, 11, 12, 14, 15, 17, 19, 29, 38, 48, 51,
54, 58, 59, 60, 61; Shutterstock pages 9, 13, 20;
Westline Publishing pages 18, 21, 25, 26, 27, 30,
31, 32, 34, 35, 40, 42, 43, 45, 52.
Illustrations on pages 9 and 47 by Mark Silver.

With many thanks to Luke Sellers for supplying the
text, and to Westline Publishing Ltd for many of the
diagrams and images.

KNOW THE GAME is a registered trademark.

Printed and bound in China by C&C Offset Printing
Co., Ltd.

Note: Throughout the book players and officials are
referred to as 'he'. This should, of course, be taken
to mean 'he or she' where appropriate.

CONTENTS

THE GAME OF CRICKET

Cricket was invented in England in the 16th century and has become one of the most widely played sports in the world. The International Cricket Council (ICC) is the world governing body for cricket, responsible for major tournaments, rules and international cricket in general. It now has more than 100 member countries and more people are playing the game than ever before. Cricket is enjoyed across the world by men and women, young and old, able-bodied people and those with disabilities.

THE ECB

The England and Wales Cricket Board (ECB) is the national governing body for the sport in England and Wales. It looks after every aspect of the game, from the playground to the Test arena.

CRICKET BASICS

Cricket is played by two teams of 11 players, although smaller-sided versions of the game are often played at junior level. Thirteen players are directly involved in the play at any one time: two batters from one team, and a bowler, wicketkeeper and nine fielders from the opposing team.

A normal one-day game is made up of two innings, which means that each team bats and bowls against the other. An innings lasts for a set amount of overs, or until 10 batters are out. The aim of the game is to score more runs than the opposition.

England's Andrew Strauss bats during a Test match.

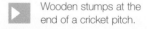
Wooden stumps at the end of a cricket pitch.

OVERS

The game of cricket is broken down into units called overs. An over consists of six legal deliveries bowled consecutively by a single bowler from the same end of the pitch.

RUNS

Points scored by the batting team are called runs, and there are three main ways a team can score them: running between the wickets, boundaries and extras.

Running between the wickets

If a batter hits the ball and runs to the opposite end of the pitch, this counts as one run (a single). If the batter then runs back to the starting end, the score is two, and so on.

A batter may run as many times as he or she likes, but must avoid being run out by the fielding team (see page 7). Both batters need to run for runs to be scored, so they cross over in the middle of the pitch. Batters can be run out if they fail to make their ground (get to the other end of the pitch).

STUMPS

The stumps are a key part of the game. One set stands at either end of the pitch, made of three vertical wooden poles 28 in (71.12cm) in height and topped by two horizontal bails.

Boundaries

The boundary refers to the perimeter of the outfield, normally marked with a rope, line or white disks. If the ball goes over the boundary without bouncing the batter automatically scores a six. If the ball makes contact with the ground after being struck and then goes over the boundary, four runs are scored.

Extras: No-balls and wides

Extras occur in a number of ways. One run is awarded to the batting team if the bowler is adjudged to have bowled a wide or a no-ball. A wide occurs when the ball is judged to be too far away from the batter to be hit with a normal shot.

The most common reason for a no-ball is when the bowler oversteps the front crease line during the delivery stride. The bowler must land with part of the foot behind the front crease line for the ball to be legal. No-balls can also be called for other reasons, such as a ball bouncing more than twice, or a ball reaching the batter above waist height without bouncing when bowled by a seam bowler, or above shoulder height from a spinner. Batters can only be out from a wide if stumped and from a no-ball if run out.

Extras: Byes and leg byes

Byes are scored when a batter runs between the wickets but has not made contact with the ball, either with the bat or with any body part. Byes are scored in the same way as normal runs, such as by running between the wickets or boundaries.

Leg byes are scored in the same way as byes except that the ball has struck the batter on the leg or other body part except for the hand. Leg byes can only be scored if the batter is trying to hit the ball with the bat or actively trying to avoid the ball. If the batter uses the leg or another part of the body to touch the ball intentionally, no run can be scored.

WAYS OF GETTING OUT

Being out means that the batter ends his or her session of play, the innings, and leaves the field.

 Cricket is normally played with a red ball, although all-day cricket now uses a white ball.

A good bowling technique is essential.

Bowled

A legal ball delivered by the bowler strikes the stumps and a bail is removed. The batter is not out if the ball fails to dislodge a bail.

Caught

The ball is caught by a fielder before it hits the ground after being struck by the batsman's bat or part of the glove.

ANOTHER BALL?

If a wide or no-ball is called, an additional ball is then bowled. However no extra ball is bowled when byes are scored.

Leg Before Wicket (LBW)

A player is out leg before wicket if the umpire judges that the ball would have hit the stumps had it not been prevented from doing so by the batter's leg pad. There are some exceptions to this rule.

A player cannot be out LBW if the ball hits the bat before the pad, or if the ball hits the pad after pitching outside leg stump, even when it would go on to hit the stumps. Also a batter is not out LBW if the ball hits the pad outside the line of the off stump provided the batter is playing a shot, even if the ball would then have hit the stumps.

Stumped

The batter leaves the crease while playing a shot, then the wicketkeeper removes a bail with the ball before the batter's foot or bat is back behind the crease line.

Run out

A player is run out if the stumps are broken by the ball when a batter is attempting to run between the wickets but is outside the crease.

Hit wicket

A bail is removed by a part of the batter's body, clothing or bat while playing a shot.

Handled the ball and obstructing the field

These are rare forms of dismissal. Players are given out handled the ball if they purposefully prevent the ball from hitting the stumps with the hand or intentionally hit the ball a second time with the bat. In obstruction, a batter purposefully prevents fielders from fielding the ball.

For the full laws of cricket visit www.lords.org/laws-and-spirit/laws-of-cricket/

UMPIRES

Cricket is traditionally played with two umpires, although all international games and many professional matches now feature a third umpire for decisions made following video replays. The umpires are responsible for making sure the laws of the game are upheld on the field, and in particular to decide when a batter is out.

One umpire stands at the bowler's end while the other stands at square leg (see page 43). They alternate positions as the bowling changes from one end to the other. The umpire at the bowler's end is responsible for major decisions and signalling runs scored. The square leg umpire is consulted in run out or stumping decisions, or any instance when this umpire has a better view than the umpire at the bowler's end.

Key umpire signals
Out
Wide
No-ball
Bye
Leg bye
Boundary 4
Boundary 6

 A cricket umpire observing play.

Umpire's Signals

The umpires communicate their decisions to the players, spectators and scorers using hand signals:

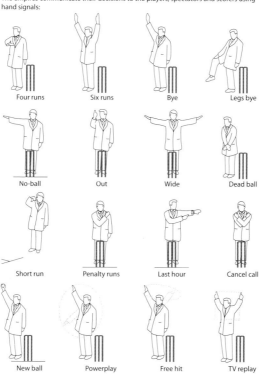

Four runs	Six runs	Bye	Legs bye
No-ball	Out	Wide	Dead ball
Short run	Penalty runs	Last hour	Cancel call
New ball	Powerplay	Free hit	TV replay

THE PITCH

Cricket is played on an oval-shaped grass field with the main action taking place on a 22-yd (20.12m) long strip in the centre, called the pitch, wicket or strip. The pitch has a set of stumps at either end and is marked with crease lines (see page 6) in front of the stumps. Junior pitches are marked in the same way but are slightly shorter in length. An Under-9s pitch is 18 yds (16.46m) long, an Under-11s pitch is 20 yds (18.29m), and an Under-13s strip is 21 yds (19.20m).

PREPARING THE PITCH

The process of preparing a pitch is very complex and requires great skill and expertise. A pitch has to be cut (mowed) and rolled precisely to ensure even bounce. Subtle differences in the way a pitch is prepared, the weather and the type of earth on which the grass grows all have significant effects on how the ball behaves and the type of game that takes place.

England's Paul Collingwood and Kevin Pieterson examine the pitch, which is being prepared prior to a Test match.

A great view of the pitch during a Test match.

THE SQUARE

Each prepared pitch is normally used only once in a season as it tends to wear and deteriorate during a game. The ground staff prepare a number of pitches alongside each other for use during the course of the season. This area of pitches is known as the square.

READING THE PITCH

A key skill for any player, particularly the captain, is to be able to read the condition of the pitch, judge how it will play and whether it will benefit batters or bowlers. Typically pitches in England have a reasonable amount of grass, are fairly slow and tend to help seam bowlers. Traditionally pitches in Australia are faster and the ball bounces more, while pitches on the Indian subcontinent tend to favour spin bowling. Of course different grounds, different countries and different climates produce varied pitches and the challenge for any player is to adapt and be successful in all conditions.

THE OUTFIELD

Surrounding the square is the area known as the outfield. This is not usually rolled and the grass is allowed to grow longer than on the pitch. The outfield requires much less preparation than the pitch. However it is important for the grass on the outfield to be kept fairly short, and the ground should be flat and even, to ensure that the ball runs quickly and smoothly across it.

THE GROUND

The most famous ground in cricket is Lord's in London, which is known as the 'Home of Cricket'. The ground is owned by the Marylebone Cricket Club (MCC) and the first game was played here in 1814. Since then the venue has seen some of the finest cricket in history, including Test matches, one-day internationals and domestic finals.

LORD'S LANDMARKS

Lord's is renowned for having a noticeable slope from one side of the playing area to the other. It also has a number of famous landmarks including the Lord's Pavilion, which contains the Long Room, and the Old Father Time weather vane. In recent years the ground has undergone massive redevelopment and features new structures, such as the eye-catching Media Centre.

For more on Lord's visit www.lords.org

The world-famous Lord's Cricket Ground.

A TYPICAL CRICKET GROUND

All cricket grounds have their own idiosyncratic features. Here are a few that are common to many of them.

Pavilion

The pavilion is at the heart of a cricket ground. It normally features the home and away team dressing rooms and is the place where meals and refreshments are taken. Many pavilions are also used as the social hub of cricket clubs, containing a bar and seating area for spectators.

Nets

Most grounds have some kind of practice area. This often takes the form of nets, which may be on an artificial surface or on grass. Nets consist of a netted area surrounding a pitch, so that bowlers can bowl at batters without the need for fielders. Most clubs use nets as part of their practice sessions.

Scorebox and scoreboard

Many grounds have a scorebox where two scorers sit. They keep a detailed record of the game in a scorebook, and they also put key information such as runs, overs and wickets on a scoreboard for players and spectators. Scoreboards can be electronic or feature numbers on rectangular pieces of wood or plastic that are put up by hand.

Equipment and shed

Most grounds have a shed, hut or similar to house the heavy roller, mower and other pieces of equipment used to prepare the ground.

SIGHTSCREENS

In most forms of cricket the sightscreens are white in colour and are usually square or rectangular. Made of wood or a synthetic material, they are situated at each end of the ground to help batters see the ball from the bowler's hand. Spectators should take care not to walk in front of a sightscreen when the bowler is bowling.

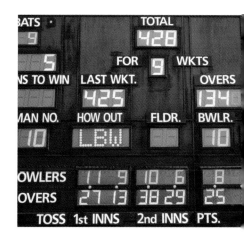

 A typical scoreboard showing runs, wickets and overs.

FORMATS OF THE GAME

Cricket is played in a number of formats that vary in length from five-day Test matches to Twenty20 games lasting a few hours. Despite the rise in popularity of shorter forms of cricket, like Twenty20 and ODs or one-day matches, Tests are still regarded as the pinnacle of the game.

TEST CRICKET

A Test match is played over five days between international teams. There are nine Test-playing countries, competing against each other home and away during a five-year cycle. A Test series can feature from one to six matches.

Test matches have two innings per team. To win, one team must score more runs than the opposition managed in two completed innings. If neither team achieves this within five days the game is drawn. A Test match can be tied if both sides are bowled out for the same aggregate score, although this has only ever happened twice in the history of the game.

Test matches are played in traditional white kit using a red ball. The ball can be changed for a new one every 80 overs. There is no time limit on how long a side may bat, but the batting captain can declare (end the innings early) if he or she feels the team has enough runs.

An English success following a Test match against the West Indies.

THE ASHES TROPHY

In the 1990s a larger Waterford crystal replica of the original Ashes urn was commissioned as a physical trophy to award to the winning team. It was first presented to victorious Australian captain Mark Taylor in 1998.

mantelpiece of his family home in Kent until his death in 1927. At his request, his wife Florence bequeathed the urn to the MCC. Today the tiny, delicate and irreplaceable artifact resides in the MCC Museum at Lord's. Each year, it is seen by tens of thousands of visitors from all parts of the world.

TEST-PLAYING NATIONS
England, Australia, Bangladesh, India, New Zealand, Pakistan, South Africa, Sri Lanka, West Indies.

The Ashes

The most famous Test series is the Ashes, contested by England and Australia. This name was born after England lost to Australia for the first time on home soil, at the Oval cricket ground in London on 29 August 1882. Next day the *Sporting Times* newspaper carried a mock obituary to English cricket, saying: 'The body will be cremated and the ashes taken to Australia.' This idea caught the public's imagination and when the English team next set off to tour Australia, captain Ivo Bligh vowed to return with 'the ashes'. Bligh's Australian counterpart, W.L. Murdoch, similarly vowed to defend them.

As well as playing three Test matches against Australia, England played many social matches. During one such game near Melbourne, on Christmas Eve 1882, Bligh was given a small terracotta urn as a symbol of 'the ashes'. Bligh saw the urn as a personal gift and it resided on the

The Ashes urn is displayed at Lord's Cricket Ground in London.

ONE-DAY CRICKET

One-day cricket is fast-paced and exciting and has become popular around the world. One-day internationals, ODIs, are played in coloured clothing with a white ball, both of which add to the spectacle of the game. The matches are characterised by attacking play, big hitting and non-stop action. The pinnacle of one-day cricket is the international World Cup, held every four years.

Number of overs

As the name suggests, one-day cricket is played over the course of a single day and is limited to a set number of overs per side. Over the years there have been many different forms of one-day cricket. The most common is 50 overs per side, which is the standard form for international games. Bowlers are limited to a maximum of 10 overs each. Captains have to adhere to certain fielding restrictions during nominated 'Powerplay' phases of the match.

POWERPLAYS

Introduced in 2005, Powerplay fielding restrictions consist of three blocks totalling 20 overs.

- During the first 10 overs, known as Powerplay 1, only two fielders may be outside the fielding circle and at least two must be in catching positions.

- Powerplay 2 and Powerplay 3 are five-over spells in which only three fielders may be outside the fielding circle, but there are no requirements about close catchers.

- The fielding side decides when to take one of these Powerplays. In a rule change introduced in October 2008, the batting side decides when the other Powerplay is taken.

England's Adi Rashid playing in a one-day tour match. Note the coloured kit and white ball.

ODI World Cups

One-day cricket was first played by English county teams in the 1960s. The inaugural World Cup was in 1971 and this competition has undergone several changes in format over the years. The current tournament is held every four years and features the best 16 international teams in the world. This includes the nine Test playing countries plus Zimbabwe and six qualifying countries.

The 2007 World Cup in the West Indies featured two groups of eight teams playing each other once (a total of seven matches for each team). The top four from each group then went forward to a 'Super 8' phase, with each team again playing seven matches, before the top four went on to the semi-finals. The 2007 final featured Australia and Sri Lanka, with the Australian team coming out on top.

COUNTY CRICKET

The top level of domestic cricket in England and Wales is played by 18 first class counties. They compete against each other in a range of competitions including Twenty20, the 40 overs-per-side Pro40 competition, and four-day county championship matches.

TWENTY20

Twenty20 cricket, the newest format, has been a huge hit with spectators. Each side bats for just 20 overs, and many games are under floodlights. Twenty20 began between English counties in 2003 and has since taken off around the world. The all-action game is played in coloured kit using a white ball, and often features music when boundaries are scored or wickets taken. The basic rules are the same as for one-day cricket but bowlers are limited to four overs each. The first Twenty20 World Cup was played in South Africa in 2007 with India crowned champions.

SENIOR CLUB CRICKET

Senior club cricket in Britain is usually an adapted form of one-day cricket. The length of the game and rules, such as the number of overs per bowler, vary from league to league. Most midweek sides play Twenty20 cricket, while weekend leagues generally play games varying from 40 to 60 overs per side.

JUNIOR CRICKET

Many youngsters get their first taste of cricket with kwik cricket or inter-cricket at school. These are simplified versions of the game to promote participation and give players their first experiences. Most club games follow two main formats: Pairs and Junior Twenty20.

Pairs cricket

Usually played by Under-11s and in some Under-13 leagues, this format is designed to maximise the involvement of young players, with two teams of eight. Each team starts with 200 runs and players bat in pairs for four overs per pair. Runs are scored in the usual way, but if a wicket is taken the batting team loses five runs and the batters swap ends rather than one of them returning to the pavilion. A bowler has a maximum of three overs, and every player must bowl at least one over, with the exception of the wicketkeeper.

 Many different skills need to be learned, including the underarm throw.

Junior Twenty20

This follows the same format as senior games, except that in many leagues batters have to retire after scoring 25 runs. They may bat again if the rest of the team is out. This is another way of ensuring that as many players as possible are involved.

OTHER FORMATS

Different formats of cricket are also played at school and representative level. Many public schools take part in timed games, where the coach decides the duration of an innings.

CRICKET ON THE NET

- England and county cricket: www.ecb.co.uk

- How to join a club, start playing cricket and other ways of getting involved: www.ecb.co.uk/ development/get-into-cricket/

- Junior formats: www.ecb.co.uk/ development/kids/

Young cricket fans cheer on their side in a junior cricket match.

EQUIPMENT

Choosing the right equipment can be a difficult task. There are so many different brands and pieces of kit available, it is hard to know what to look for. The key to choosing any equipment is that you find it comfortable. Everyone has different budgets and preferences, but here are a few handy guidelines to help you choose equipment that will be comfortable and fit well.

CLOTHING

Cricket is traditionally played in white clothing and this is still the colour worn in Test matches, county championship games and in most recreational cricket. White was initially chosen to make the red ball easier to see for the batsman. In the professional game teams now wear coloured kit for limited-overs cricket where a white ball is used.

BATS

Cricket bats are made from willow. A full-size bat typically weighs from 2 lb 5 oz to 3 lb (1.05 to 1.36kg) and is restricted to 38 in (96.5cm) in length. The bat is shaped like a paddle, with the flat face for striking the ball. The handle is made from wood or carbon fibre and is 'sprung' with rubber, cork or a combination of both. It is then bound with string and covered

with a rubber grip. The best cricket bats are made by hand, with master bat-makers using traditional methods that have been around for generations.

▶ Your cricket bat should be the correct size and weight.

Choosing a bat

The bat is the main tool of your trade, so choosing the right one is really important. The most significant things to consider are the size and weight. Some young players buy bats to 'grow into' but this is harmful for developing good technique. A bat that is too big will hamper your ability to play certain shots.

Bat size

A reasonable way to find the right bat size is to stand up straight with a bat by your side. The handle of the bat should reach the top of your thigh. Bats range from size one to six for young players and include the harrow, which is between size six and an adult, short-handle bat. Most senior players use short-handle bats but long handles are also available.

The quality of a bat depends on the grade of willow and is reflected in the price, which ranges from £70 to £300 or more for an adult size.

LOOKING AFTER YOUR BAT

To get the best from your bat, several procedures are recommended by manufacturers. They include knocking in the bat – hitting the bat face with a cricket ball or wooden 'bat mallet' to prepare it for action. Knocking in conditions and hardens the surface of the bat, improves the 'middle' and helps to give the bat a longer life.

The correct stance and a good bat are vital to success.

Bat weight

The most common mistake people make when buying a bat is to choose one that is too heavy. Many young players want to emulate their heroes, such as England's Andrew Flintoff, who is known to use a heavy bat. A bat that is too heavy will limit the range of shots you can play. A good way to test if a bat is light enough is to pick it up using your top hand only (the upper hand when you grip the bat ready to play). If you are able to take a good backswing and demonstrate both straight and cross-batted shots with just one hand then the bat is light enough.

Pads provide protection, but are light enough to be able to run in.

THE BALL

Cricket balls have a core of cork covered by tightly wound string. The outer cover is four quarters of leather. Two of these quarters are held together by a stitched, raised seam that runs over the 'equator' of the ball while the other two are tightly pressed together.

Cricket balls are traditionally dyed red but white balls are now frequently used in limited-overs cricket and Tests have even been carried out using fluorescent pink balls.

FOOTWEAR

Cricket boots are usually made from leather and have metal spikes on the sole for grip. Some boots have rubber grips or a half-rubber, half-spiked sole. The boot itself is lightweight and provides support and shock absorption. It must also be robust enough to provide some protection if a player is struck on the foot by the ball.

PADS

Pads are made of lightweight foam material. They should be big enough to cover above the knee on each leg, but it is important they are not too big as this will cause difficulty when running between the wickets. Pads are fastened using velcro straps. They should be secured so that the end of the strap is on the outside of the leg, and tightly enough that they do not slip during running but not too tight as to be uncomfortable. Most pads become more comfortable the more they are worn, as they gradually mould to your legs. The best pads provide good protection but are also lightweight, to be comfortable and make it easy to run between the wickets.

BOWLING BOOTS

Some fast bowlers favour bowling boots. This style of boot covers the ankle and has much greater support to deal with the extra force a bowler places on the foot and ankle area. Ideally a boot should be lightweight while offering maximum support.

A cricket ball for adults weighs 5.5 oz (171g). Juniors play with a 4.75 oz (147.7g) ball until they reach Under-14 level.

GLOVES

There are many different styles of gloves available but most are made with a combination of lightweight foam and leather. When trying on gloves make sure your fingers fill them but do not press hard against the end. It should be comfortable to fasten the glove securely around the wrist.

Gloves have extra protection on the thumb of the bottom hand (the lower hand when you grip the bat ready to play), which is the left hand for left-handers and right for right-handers. Gloves should provide protection but also allow the hand and fingers to flex and bend. The more gloves are worn, the easier they become to flex.

Inners

Some batters like to wear inners when they bat. These are thin cotton gloves worn under batting gloves, for comfort and sweat absorption. If you usually wear inners, make sure that you try on gloves with inners before purchasing them.

HELMETS

It is now a law of the game for players under 18 years of age to wear a helmet when batting unless they have written permission from a parent or guardian to go without. Although batting in a helmet may feel uncomfortable at first, it is advisable for all young players to wear one.

The helmet should fit snugly to the head and is usually fastened by a velcro chin strap which can be adjusted. If the helmet has a grille then make sure that you can see clearly between the visor and the top of the grille when you take up your normal stance, ready to face the bowler. Grilles can also be adjusted but ensure that the gap between the grille and the visor is narrow enough to prevent a cricket ball passing through. Remember that the ball may be travelling fast as it hits this gap, so the grille should be firm and secure.

 A young player demonstrating good positioning for the straight drive.

All cricket clubs should have helmets to borrow, but it is better to have your own so that you can adjust it to fit you properly.

HELMET DAMAGE

If you are struck on the head by a cricket ball, or drop your helmet on a hard floor, it is advisable to get it checked out. If a helmet sustains significant damage after an impact it may no longer provide the necessary protection and will have to be replaced.

Wearing the correct gear is essential for wicketkeeping practice.

This player is wearing pads and a helmet for protection.

OTHER EQUIPMENT

There are various other pieces of protective equipment that can be purchased, although not all are necessary.

Box

It is vital for boys and men to wear a box at all times when facing a hard ball. The box is inexpensive and every player should have his own. To wear a box, players must have the right underwear; boxer shorts will not work. It is best to use briefs or special cricket shorts that can be bought from cricket and sports shops.

Thigh pads

It helps young players to get used to wearing a front thigh pad, though it is not usually necessary until about Under-13 level. A blow on the thigh is not usually dangerous but can be very painful. When buying a thigh pad, ensure that it covers the area between the top of the front pad and the waist, but it is not so big that it affects movement. Inner thigh guards can also be bought but these are not essential. Most players go without the inner thigh guard until they start playing senior cricket.

Arm guards and chest guards

These types of guards are also available but are normally only worn when batting on a bouncy surface or against particularly fast bowling.

WICKETKEEPING GEAR

Due to the wicketkeeper's exposed position, handling almost every ball bowled and coping with the speed of fast bowlers, there are special types of equipment available.

Gloves

Wicketkeeping gloves are made from leather and have a dimpled rubber surface on the palm to help catch the ball. Gloves need to be lightweight and provide cushioning to protect the hands from being bruised by the impact of the ball. Gloves contain a webbed area between thumb and index finger; the size of this area is regulated by the International Cricket Council. Most wicketkeepers wear inners underneath their main gloves to provide extra protection and absorb sweat.

Pads

Wicketkeeping pads are smaller and lighter than batting pads. They come up to just over the knee but are designed to make sure they do not inhibit the wicketkeeper's movement when crouching in the stance. Like batting pads, they are designed to protect against the ball but should be comfortable and lightweight.

Under ECB regulation all wicketkeepers under 18 years of age must wear a helmet when standing up to the stumps, unless they have parental or guardian consent to go without.

 A helmet is a vital piece of safety equipment.

BATTING

To win any game of cricket a team must score more runs than the opposition. That's the simple part. How you score runs, which shots you play and the way you play is all down to the individual. Every batter has his or her personal style but there are a few key skills shared by all top players.

ESSENTIAL SKILLS

All batters should have a sound technique, good decision-making and be able to concentrate for long periods of time. Batters should be comfortable playing on the front foot or back foot and be able to adapt the way they play to the match situation and the type of bowling they face. As you can see, many things go towards making a top batter. Here are a few simple techniques to help you on your way.

A crucial part of batting is the batter's set-up. Your grip, stance and backswing affect every shot you play. If you get these simple things right you will avoid many common problems faced by batters and it will help you master the whole range of shots. While many individual batting set-ups may be subtly different, there are a few key points that most have in common.

TYPES OF BATTERS

- Openers – batters at the top of the order, numbers 1 and 2.
- Middle order, numbers 3 to 7
- Tailenders, numbers 8 to 11.
- Allrounder – a player who is equally adept as a batter and a bowler.
- Night watchman – a tailender who goes in further up the order towards the end of a day's play, so that the specialist batters do not have to go in with only a few overs left. The night watchman's job is simply to avoid getting out so the specialist batter is protected until the following day. This tactic is only used in Test matches or four-day county games.

England's Matt
Prior in to bat.

Grip

When gripping the bat you should have both hands together in the middle of the handle. Your strongest hand should be at the bottom (right hand for right-handers and vice versa) and your weaker hand on top. Notice how the index finger and thumb of each hand form a 'V' shape. The V on each hand should be in line halfway between the outside edge of the bat and the splice.

Stance

A batter's stance should be comfortable and balanced. Ensure that your head is still and your eyes are level as you prepare to face the ball. Your feet should be in line with each other, parallel to the crease. You should feel balanced so that you are able to more forward or back, depending on the ball you are facing.

Backswing

When picking up or lifting the bat backwards to play a shot, you should make sure you take the bat back in a straight line. The bat should be raised a little higher than the stumps to help you make a powerful strike. It is important to pick up the bat using your arms rather than your hands as this will help you take a smooth, powerful swing. The backswing should happen at the same time as you take your first step to get into position, ready to play the ball.

FRONT FOOT SHOTS

Batting strokes can be divided into front foot shots and back foot shots. Front foot shots are usually played to balls that are full in length and include the straight drive, cover drive and on drive, and the forward defensive shot.

Front foot drive

A great way to improve your front foot shots is to practise the front foot drive. Although the drive is an attacking shot it shares many similarities with the forward defensive as well. The drive is played to a full ball known as a half-volley. It is a powerful shot requiring a full swing of the bat.

 Your stance should be comfortable and balanced.

- First move your head and leading shoulder towards the ball.

- Your front foot should follow the movement of your head and shoulder so you take a good stride towards the ball.

- Take a full backswing to ensure you can hit the ball powerfully.

- Strike the ball with a straight (vertical) bat, using the full face and following through over your shoulder.

 This player demonstrates a good technique for driving practice.

Driving practice

This practice can be done in a small group or on your own. Place a ball on a golf tee (if you do not have a tee, a plastic cup can do the same job). Set up a 'goal' with a width of 4–5 yds (4–5m) a minimum of 12 yds (11m) from the ball, using handy items such as road cones or coats. If you are in a group, place fielders in the goal to act as 'goalkeepers' and field the ball.

Take your stance a little way back from the ball, so you have to step towards it to play the drive. Attempt to strike the ball along the ground and into the goal. Have a few goes and then swap with your team-mates.

You can change the drill by moving the goal to one side or the other to practise your cover drives and on drives. These shots are similar to the front foot drive but played to balls of slightly differing lines. The cover drive is played to a full-length ball outside off stump and is hit through the cover/extra cover area (see page 43). The on drive is played to a full length ball pitching in line with middle and leg stumps and is hit between midwicket and mid-on (see page 43).

GET COMPETITIVE: DRIVING

- If you want to make driving practice more competitive you can bring in points for scoring a 'goal'.

- To make the practice harder you can alter the 'feed' of the ball to you. For example, the next step after hitting from a tee is to have someone, the 'feeder', drop the ball just in front of you. Use a tennis ball and aim to strike it on the second or third bounce.

- For the next stage, the 'feeder' throws the ball underarm, making sure it bounces two to three times before reaching you. This is known as a bobble feed and increases the difficulty of the shot since you are now facing a moving ball.

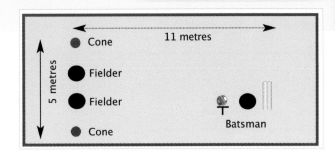

A set-up for batting practice. Make sure the fielders are a safe distance away.

Forward defensive

The technique for playing a forward defensive shot is similar to the drive. Instead of hitting the ball powerfully and following through, you allow the bat to stop as it hits the ball. This results in the ball dropping down near to the wicket.

> As the batter takes stance, the off side is the side where the bat is (the right for a right-hander), while the leg or on side is the side of the legs.

BACK FOOT SHOTS

Back foot shots are played to balls that are pitched shorter than a good length. They include the back foot defensive, back foot drive, cut, pull and hook shots.

Footwork

One of the key skills of playing short pitch bowling well is to have good footwork. For back foot shots this means taking a step back and across towards off stump, making sure you use the full depth of the crease. This will give you more time to play the ball and help you get on top of the bounce and hit the ball down.

Good positioning for the front foot defensive.

The pull

One of the most common back foot shots is the pull. The main coaching points for a right-hander (reversed for a left-hander) are as follows.

- Move your back foot backwards and across towards off stump, keeping it parallel with the batting crease.

- Take a big backswing, ensuring your hands are higher than the ball.

- Bring your front foot back and towards the left side, making you chest-on to the ball.

- Keeping your head still, hit down into the ball with a horizontal bat.

- Transfer body weight from your back leg to the front leg.

- Follow through with your bat finishing over your front shoulder and in a balanced position.

Pulling practice

Place a tee on top of a stump about 1–2 ft (0.3–0.5m) outside the batting crease in line with middle and leg stumps. Place a 'goal' (see page 32) square – that is, at right angles to the pitch – on the leg side about 15 yds (15m) from the batter. The batter strikes the ball off the tee and through the goal.

GET COMPETITIVE: PULLING

- Make the goal smaller and add points for goals scored.

- Replace the stump and tee with a feeder, who stands about 11 yds (11m) away and throws the ball overarm to bounce about 3 yds (3m) from the batter. The batter must now take into account the bounce of the ball and the slight variations in line that occur with a feeder, which makes the drill more difficult.

The pull is a common shot for a batsman.

RUNNING BETWEEN THE WICKETS

A crucial part of batting is running between the wickets. This is the ability to judge when runs are available and communicate with your partner to help keep the scoreboard ticking over. To avoid confusion, a batter should make one of three calls when looking for a run.

- 'Yes' if wanting to run.

- 'No' if not wanting to run.

- 'Wait', swiftly followed by 'Yes' or 'No', if initially unsure that there is a run available.

The batter who hits the ball is responsible for the call unless the ball goes behind the stumps. Then the non-striker should call as it is easier for him or her to see. The non-striker's other job is to back up, which means starting to walk down the wicket as the bowler releases the ball, ready to run.

BATTING RECORDS

- Indian batsman Sachin Tendulkar is the highest run scorer in Test match history with more than 12,000 runs.

- West Indian batter Brian Lara scored most runs in a single Test innings with 400 not out versus England in 2004.

BOWLING

A bowler has two main roles. One is to try and limit the batsmen's scoring and the other is to take wickets. Often these two roles go hand in hand as a tight spell of bowling can put batters under pressure and force them to make mistakes.

TYPES OF BOWLERS

There are two main types of bowler – seam bowlers such as England's James Anderson, and spinners such as Monty Panesar. Seam bowlers generally bowl faster than spinners and move the ball through the air by swing or off the pitch using seam movement. Spinners make the ball move off the pitch by putting spin on the ball with the fingers or wrist. The key to success as a seamer or a spinner is to match good control with movement and an element of deception.

BOWLING BASICS

All bowlers will have actions that are subtly different, but there are also many similarities.

Run-up
All bowlers should have a smooth, rhythmical approach to the wicket.

Take-off
Bowlers should look to take off from the non-bowling foot (left foot for right-handers, right foot for left-arm bowlers).

Back foot contact
Bowlers should land on the opposite foot to the one from which they took off. At this point they should have the front arm raised and the head still, looking towards the target.

Front foot contact
As the bowler's front foot hits the ground the bowling arm should be brought over, keeping it straight, to release the ball when the arm is just past the vertical. The head should be upright, looking at the target.

Follow through
After releasing the ball the seam bowler should allow the body to keep moving towards the target until it comes to a natural stop. A spin bowler's follow though is slightly different as it involves pivoting through 180 degrees on the front foot rather than continuing down the wicket.

THE STOCK BALL

While most bowlers have a number of different types of delivery, it is important to master your 'stock ball' before trying to bowl too many variations. That means being able consistently to bowl the off-break if you are an off-spinner or the out-swinger if you are a swing bowler. Many top bowlers vary their pace and the type of swing, spin or seam movement they produce, but the key to these variations being successful is to first have a good stock ball.

Back foot contact with the front arm still raised.

Front foot contact. Notice the straight bowling arm just about to release the ball.

SWING AND BOWLING

One of the main weapons in a seam bowler's armoury is swing. This is where the ball curves through the air either away from or into the batter. It is achieved by a good wrist position and is enhanced by having one side of the ball shinier than the other. There are two main types of swing, out-swing and in-swing.

Out-swing

If a right-arm bowler bowls an out-swinger or away-swinger to a right-handed batter, the ball will move in the air away from the batter, towards the off side.

The orthodox grip is to have your first two fingers either side of the seam with the side of your thumb on the seam underneath the ball. Try and keep the ball towards the end of the fingers. You should have the shiny side of the ball on the right and the seam slightly angled towards the off side.

In-Swing

A right-arm bowler will swing a ball towards a right-handed batter, that is, from off to leg, when bowling the in-swinger.

Grip the ball with your first two fingers close together either side of the seam with the flat part of your thumb on the seam underneath the ball. It can help to have your fingers more on top of the ball than for the out-swinger. You need to have the shiny side of the ball on the left, with the seam slightly angled in the direction you wish to swing the ball.

 Paul Collingwood during a practice session.

BOWLING STRAIGHT

If you do not wish to swing the ball, the basic grip is similar to the ones described above. Simply hold the ball in the same way but with your fingers running in a straight line either side of the seam at the top and the side of your thumb on the seam underneath, as shown below.

BOWLING RECORDS

- English bowler Jim Laker took a record 19 wickets in the Test match against Australia at Manchester in 1956.
- Sri Lankan spinner Muttiah Muralitharan, who has a controversial bent-arm bowling action, has taken more than 750 Test match wickets. Shane Warne is in second place on 708.

A basic bowling grip.

LINE AND LENGTH

All bowlers need good control over their line and length.

- Line refers to the direction of the ball.
- Length refers to where the ball pitches (hits the ground) on the pitch.

- Most bowlers should start by learning to bowl a good length on a line of off stump or just outside.
- The line and length a bowler chooses will vary depending on swing, seam, spin, the pace and bounce of the wicket and the batter's strengths and weaknesses.

 A guide to bowling length.

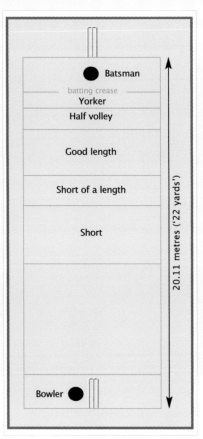

 A set-up for bowling practice.

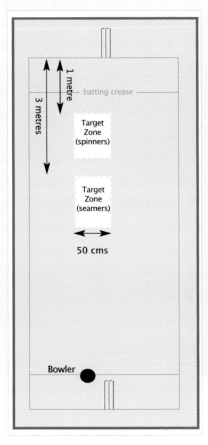

SPIN BOWLING

Spin is imparted by the fingers or the wrist as the ball is released, making the ball move off the pitch. Off-spin is produced using the fingers and makes the ball move from off to leg, towards a right-handed batter. Leg spin is produced using a flick of the wrist and turns from leg to off, away from a right-handed batter.

Off-spin grip

The orthodox grip for off-spin is to grip the ball with the first two fingers, with the first joints of these fingers spread widely on the seam. The thumb should not be in contact with the ball. Spin is imparted mainly by the first finger and through turning your wrist clockwise as though opening a door.

Leg-spin grip

The orthodox grip for leg spin is a two-finger grip. The top joints of the first two fingers lie across the seam with the third finger bent along the seam. The thumb should remain off the ball. Spin is imparted by the third finger and a flick of the wrist. You should flick your wrist anti-clockwise so the ball is released from the back of the hand.

PRACTICE

A good practice for any type of bowler is a simple target bowling exercise. Set up a target area on the line or the length where you want to bowl, and practise landing the ball there consistently. To make the practice more challenging you can make the target area smaller or move it to different lines and lengths.

If the ball is polished so that one side is smoother and shinier than the other, and then bowled correctly, the shinier side causes less air friction and so the ball swings to that side.

FIELDING

Most players spend more time fielding during a game than doing anything else, so being a good fielder is a vital part of being a successful cricketer. Good fielding can stop the batting side scoring and help take wickets through catches, run-out chances and putting the batter under pressure. It is important to be able to field in as many areas as possible to be a real asset to the team.

CLOSE CATCHERS

Close catchers include slip and gully fielders, and positions in front of the wicket such as forward short leg and silly point. Their most important job is to take any catches that come their way.

Key attributes and skills

Close catchers need to have great hands, good reactions and be able to concentrate for long periods of time. They should be agile and able to dive to take a catch. A vital skill is to catch the ball consistently even though it is likely to be travelling at speed and could come at any height.

Coaching points

- When waiting for the ball, have your legs a comfortable distance apart with your knees slightly bent so you are in a balanced position.

- Try to catch the ball with both hands, with your fingers pointing down and your head over the ball.

- As you take the ball, keep watching it and 'give' slightly with your hands to stop the ball bouncing out.

A good fielder needs excellent reactions and to maintain concentration for long periods of time.

RING FIELDERS

Positions for ring fielders include cover, point, square leg, midwicket, mid-on and mid-off. They must be versatile and perform a number of different tasks. Their jobs are to stop the batter scoring runs, take catches, perform run-outs, chase the ball to the boundary if the ball should pass them, and back up other fielders. They should throw to the top of the stumps so it is easy for the bowler or wicketkeeper to take, unless the situation means throwing directly at the stumps.

Key attributes and skills

Ring fielders should be quick, agile and well-balanced. They need to be able to throw accurately overarm and underarm and be comfortable attacking the ball or stopping a well-struck shot. Ring fielders should also be good at catching both high balls and flatter, more powerful strikes. A key skill is the one-handed intercept and underarm throw. It is performed at speed when the ball is rolling along the ground, to try and stop the batter taking a single or to claim a run-out.

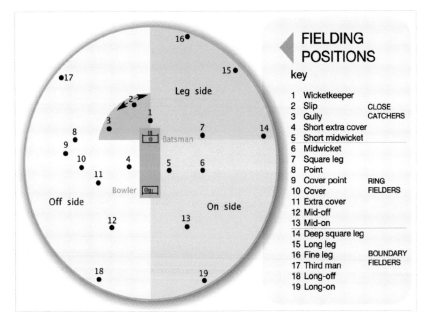

FIELDING POSITIONS

key

1	Wicketkeeper	
2	Slip	
3	Gully	CLOSE CATCHERS
4	Short extra cover	
5	Short midwicket	
6	Midwicket	
7	Square leg	
8	Point	
9	Cover point	RING FIELDERS
10	Cover	
11	Extra cover	
12	Mid-off	
13	Mid-on	
14	Deep square leg	
15	Long leg	
16	Fine leg	BOUNDARY FIELDERS
17	Third man	
18	Long-off	
19	Long-on	

Leg side
Batsman
Bowler
Off side
On side

Coaching points

- For the one-handed intercept and underarm throw, attack the ball at speed in a balanced position, low to the ground.

- Pick up the ball outside your throwing foot (the foot on the same side as the arm you throw with), your fingers pointing down and your palm facing the ball.

- Staying low, move your head up to look at target.

- Point your non-throwing arm at the target and throw underarm at it.

- After release, keep your throwing arm moving across your body, finishing with your hand near to your other hand – if you are right-handed, the right hand should finish by your left hip.

- This skill is best practised in pairs. One player rolls the ball out and acts as wicketkeeper while the other performs the one-handed intercept and throw.

BOUNDARY FIELDERS

As the name suggests, these positions involve fielders in the 'deep', protecting the boundary. Positions include fine leg, third man, long-on, long-off, deep backward square leg and deep cover. A boundary fielder's main job is to stop the ball going for four or six. Boundary fielders also take high catches when batters play attacking shots, and stay on their toes to stop batters taking twos and threes.

Key attributes
Boundary fielders should have a good overarm throw, be quick over the ground and agile enough to throw themselves full length to stop a boundary. They also need to be able to take high catches.

Coaching points
A key skill for all boundary fielders is a powerful and accurate overarm throw.

- Holding the ball across the seam, take a long straight stride towards the target so you are balanced and sideways on to the target.

- Point your front arm at the target and pull back your throwing arm.

- Make an L shape with your throwing arm ensuring the elbow is level with or above your shoulder.

- As your chest faces the target, drive your front arm forwards and release the ball from a low position with your legs bent.

- Your front arm should follow through across your body as your back leg comes through and round.

- Keep your head still and eyes level, looking at the target throughout the movement.

This sequence shows the different stages of a standing throw.

THROWING PRACTICE

A good way to practise the overarm throw is simply to draw a target on a wall and try to hit it consistently. As you become more confident you can move farther from the wall or change the size of the target.

WICKETKEEPING

Being a wicketkeeper is a tough but crucial job. As a keeper you are always in the thick of the action, and must have great concentration as well as good agility and safe hands. You might go for long periods without any chances coming your way – and then be called upon to take a vital catch or stumping that could change the outcome of the match.

KEY ATTRIBUTES

As a wicketkeeper you must be comfortable against fast bowlers and standing up (near) to the stumps for spinners. Wicketkeepers must be able to read the type of ball being bowled and work out whether it will spin, swing, bounce or keep low. It is also the wicketkeeper's job to keep the fielders focused, offering encouragement and showing energy and enthusiasm.

WICKETKEEPER'S STANCE

The wicketkeeper's stance should be crouched in a comfortable and balanced position. The stance should allow you to move to either side to take a low or high ball.

The wicketkeeper moves to the side to take the ball.

TAKING THE BALL

- Stay low and move up as you take the ball.

- Give with your hands and take the ball under your head.

- If the ball is below waist height you should have your hands together and fingers pointing down.

- When taking a high ball some wicketkeepers reverse their hands, while others try and take the ball with their fingers parallel to the ground.

Practice

A simple practice that can be done standing up or back involves a 'feeder' throwing the ball so it bounces on a good length. The feeder varies the line so that you take the ball to both the off and leg sides.

When you are comfortable with this practice you can bring a batter in front of the stumps. The batter will distract you and obscure your line of vision by playing shots but just missing the ball each time.

KEEPING RECORDS

- South Africa keeper Mark Boucher has taken more Test dismissals than any other player, with more than 450.

- England's Jack Russell holds the record for most dismissals in a Test match, taking 11 against South Africa in 1995.

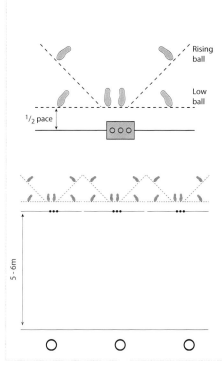

A set-up showing foot positioning for wicketkeeping practice.

CAPTAINCY

Being a captain in cricket is one of the toughest jobs in sport. The captain is responsible for choosing whether to bat or bowl, setting fields, picking the batting order and deciding who should bowl. The captain needs to give team-mates support and confidence and be a good decision-maker, a skilled communicator and keep a cool head under pressure.

TOSSING UP

As captain, if you win the toss of the coin then you decide whether your team will bat or field first. Important considerations include the pitch and the weather. If the pitch is damp and the ball is likely to swing, you may choose to bowl first; if it is a hard, even pitch and a hot day, it may be best to bat. The decision is also based on the strengths and weaknesses of your own team and your knowledge of the opposition.

BATTING ORDER

You need to pick a well balanced order that plays to the strengths of individual batters. It is a good idea to try and have a settled batting line-up so players are aware of the roles they are expected to play.

BOWLERS

When choosing who should bowl and when to make a bowling change, it is important to speak to the bowlers. You need to understand your bowlers and the pitch conditions. You also need to read the strengths and weaknesses of the opposition batters, to decide which bowler will be most effective against each of them. You need to be able to read the game and decide whether you are more likely to take wickets through attacking or by building pressure. You should also consider when your bowlers will become fatigued and how to use their overs allowance in limited-overs matches.

SETTING FIELDS

It is important to place fielders in the areas where the batters are most likely to hit the ball if the bowler is consistent in line and length. You must also adapt to the way batters play and the state of the game. If you are looking to attack, you may want more fielders in catching positions; if you are defending, you may put more players on the boundary. Often the best field is a combination of the two. You also need to put your best fielders in the most important positions where they can use their skills to advantage.

TEAM SPIRIT

A good captain promotes team spirit and keeps players motivated. This may be done in team talks off and on the field, and by talking to players regularly and helping them with any problems.

The captain should always keep talking to central players such as the bowlers, wicketkeeper and vice-captain about key decisions.

The England captain Andrew Strauss speaks to the team during a training session.

FITNESS

Modern-day cricketers need to be athletes, and being fit and healthy helps you to get the most out of the game. Top players need to be fit enough to perform successfully over long periods of time without being affected by fatigue or injury. Being fit will help you hit the ball farther, stop more runs in the field and bowl faster and for longer.

PHYSICAL FITNESS

To improve your physical fitness, it's best to consult your coach first, to help you create a programme suited to your individual needs.

Endurance

Endurance, also known as stamina, is the ability to keep going over a long period of time, such as a day's play. Having good endurance helps you to stay focused and stops you becoming tired when fielding or batting. It also helps you recover more quickly from shorter bursts of activity. Examples of ways to improve endurance include gentle jogging for 25 minutes (junior players) or 35–40 minutes (adults) several times a week, or by swimming or cycling for the same amounts of time.

Strength and power

Being strong and powerful will help you to perform skills such as striking a ball hard, bowling fast and taking off to make a diving catch.

Strength and power can be easily improved by doing exercises using your own body as resistance. Exercises such as press-ups, tricep dips and core work help your strength and are unlikely to cause injury.

USING WEIGHTS

Any fitness work with weights should only be done when you have stopped growing and after consultation with a physiotherapist, fitness trainer or experienced coach.

You must work on your fitness to remain agile. Dimitri Mascarenhas demonstrates here during a nets session.

Speed
Being fast helps you to run between the wickets and get to the ball quicker in the field. Speed can be improved by practising sprinting over short distances, such as the length of a pitch, or by shuttle runs (to and fro) of varying distances.

Agility
Being agile helps you to be light on your feet and is important for a whole range of skills, including fielding, bowling and batting footwork. There are many kinds of practices to improve agility, such as performing sprints over courses that include a number of tight turns, or using a ladder on the ground to encourage fast footwork.

Flexibility
Flexibility is important to help prevent injury. It is vital for fast bowlers, who put great strain on their bodies during their action. Flexibility can be improved by a whole range of static stretches and is best done after exercise. Hold each stretch for 30 seconds and repeat two or three times, to help increase your range of movement.

For more on static stretches visit www.cricket secrets.com/ warmingup.html

WARM-UP AND COOL-DOWN

Players should get into the habit of taking part in a warm-up and cool-down before and after each session. A warm-up gets the body ready for activity and includes a range of cricket skills and dynamic stretches. A cool-down contains a gradual decrease in intensity and includes static stretches to help the body's recovery from exercise. (For more on warm-ups and cool-downs see page 55.)

LIFESTYLE

Key mental skills are coupled with maintaining a balanced lifestyle. Young players often have to juggle cricket with their studies and other commitments, which can be difficult.
It is important to organise yourself to make sure you have time to play, practise, study, rest and relax.

NUTRITION

It is important for players to eat a healthy balanced diet that contains carbohydrates, proteins, vitamins and fibre but is low in saturated fat. For example, foods such as pasta, rice and baked potatoes are good sources of energy, while deep-fried foods and fast food should only make up a very small part of your diet as they are high in saturated fat.

Before, during and after games it is important to keep up energy levels and take on fluids to avoid dehydration. Becoming dehydrated and fatigued can make you feel unwell and have a detrimental effect on performance. Drinks breaks are built into matches, but it is worth keeping a bottle of water near the boundary, especially at third man or fine leg if you are a bowler. Batters are entitled to ask the umpires if they may take a drinks break during an innings.

MENTAL FITNESS

As well as being physically fit, cricketers need to be mentally strong. Many coaches believe the difference between top international players and good club cricketers is often down to their mastery of the mental side of the game. This can be broken down into four key areas known as the Four Cs: concentration, control, confidence and commitment.

Concentration
Cricketers need to be able to concentrate for long periods of time and remain focused even after bowling a bad ball, playing and missing with the bat, or misfielding.

Control
This refers to staying cool and calm under pressure. Top players are able to keep control of their emotions even at times of intense pressure.

Confidence
The ability to keep believing in yourself is vital, even after injury or poor performance. Confident players are willing to take risks to gain success and pick themselves up quickly when things do not go their way.

Commitment
Commitment allows players to persevere with new techniques under pressure or continue to pursue personal goals.

Cricket skills can be incorporated in the warm-up session to get the body ready for the activity to follow.

THE DAY OF THE GAME

A game of cricket can last anywhere between three hours for a Twenty20 match to five days for a Test. One of the challenges facing players is how to make sure they are mentally and physically ready whenever they are called into action. Using a one-day game as an example, these are some of the key periods during a day's play.

PRE-MATCH

It may sound like a basic step, but it is crucial your kit bag is packed with everything you will need for the day's play. Make sure you have the right clothing and footwear to deal with different weather and pitch conditions. Items such as boot spikes, sunscreen and a hat should never leave your kit bag.

It is also vital to have enough food and drink to get through the day, as fatigue and dehydration will have a big impact on performance. The best option to stay hydrated is to keep drinking water throughout the day. While it is a good idea to eat a high-energy meal such as pasta before a game, many players keep topping up energy levels through the day with items such as bananas, energy bars or sweets.

The weather can have an important influence of the outcome of a game.

WARM-UP

Get to the ground in time for a thorough warm-up. This will normally be run by the coach or captain but you should be aware of the sorts of exercises that you need to do to prepare for the match. A good warm-up should get you ready for the game both physically and mentally, including routines such as dynamic stretches and skills practices.

This is also the time when you may want to look at the pitch, try and work out how it will play, and choose from which end to bowl. A full warm-up typically takes between 45 minutes and an hour, and it includes time for players to prepare individually as well as a team talk.

CRICKET AND THE WEATHER

A game of cricket can be heavily influenced by the weather. When deciding whether to bat or bowl first, it is useful to be aware of the weather conditions and how they may affect the game. Hot, dry weather normally favours batting first while overcast, humid conditions help swing bowling. Reading these conditions can be a real asset to your team.

For more on dynamic stretches and warming up visit www.cricket secrets.com/ warmingup.html

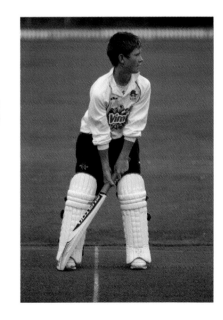

 It is vital players warm up adequately.

DURING THE GAME

Throughout the game it is important to watch the action closely. Whether you are batting or fielding, try to work out factors such as run rate (the number of runs a team is scoring per over), what the bowlers are doing, and how the pitch is playing, as this will help you and your team-mates.

- Fielders – support your team-mates and keep your concentration.
- Bowlers – make sure you are loose and ready whenever the captain needs you.
- Batting team – stay together, support the batters and be ready to bat before you go in.

THE INTERVAL

Take on plenty of fluid and some food. The coach or captain may bring the team together to discuss how to chase or defend the target. If you are opening the batting or bowling next, make sure you prepare in good time, such as facing throw-downs or bowling a few practice deliveries.

POST-MATCH

At the end of the game it is important to thank the opposition and umpires and shake their hands regardless of the result. Take part in a cool-down, which should include static stretching to ensure your muscles do not become stiff.

Following a match, the coach or captain often leads a reflection of the game, drawing on the positives and bringing out areas to improve.

PLAYER PROGRESS

For young players aiming for the very top there is a clear pathway through the grades and ages. Working hard and achieving success at each level in turn will earn you the recognition to keep moving forward in your development. In particular, a key phase for youngsters is to test skills against adult players. Many top youngsters start playing senior cricket at their clubs from around the age of 14 years.

PREPARING TO BAT AND BOWL

- Throw-downs involve a team-mate or coach throwing the ball to a batter to help the batter hone shots before an innings.
- Practising bowling deliveries should be done using a full-length pitch and can include marked target areas.

Finding the right club is an important step in every player's development. To find a club in your area visit www.ecb.play-cricket.com

SELF ANALYSIS

At some point after each game, it is a good process to reflect on your performance. Pick out what you have done well and what you would like to develop, learn from your experiences and ensure that you keep improving your game.

A player is practising with throw-downs prior to batting.

FAIR PLAY

Cricket is renowned for promoting good sportsmanship and fair play. The phrase 'it's just not cricket' refers to the game's strong ideals that hold sporting behaviour in the highest regard. Every player taking the field at any level is responsible for upholding cricket's reputation for fair play.

RESPECT

It is important to respect the rights, dignity and worth of every person involved in cricket. Even in the most competitive matches it is crucial to behave in a respectful and sporting way to opponents, officials and spectators. This means not questioning an umpire's decision and not 'sledging' (verbally abusing) fellow players and supporters. An example of respect is the tradition of shaking the hands of opponents and officials at the end of the game.

TREAT EVERYONE EQUALLY

Cricket is a truly global game played by people from many different cultures, races, ethnicities and religions, by people of all ages and backgrounds, male and female, and by people with disabilities. It is important that no one is discriminated against on any of these grounds. Such behaviour should never go unchallenged.

Find out more about the One Game campaign and pledge at www.ecb.co.uk/ecb/one-game/one-game-pledge/

Cricket attracts huge crowds from many backgrounds. It is important for competitive matches to be played in the spirit of the game.

FAIRNESS

Every player should maintain integrity and never try to influence a game through dishonesty or deception. Participants should learn and adhere to the laws of the game, and encourage colleagues to do the same. Players, coaches, officials and supporters should encourage performance as well as results. This means recognising good performances by players regardless of their team and the match result.

BEHAVIOUR

Participants should maintain high standards of behaviour throughout a game, regardless of result, performance or decisions.

As the current guardians of cricket, it is up to each and every one of us to hand our game on in better shape that when we found it. This philosophy applies at all levels of the game from the playground through to international teams.

THE ONE GAME INITIATIVE

- The ECB One Game initiative promotes cricket's sporting values.

- An important part is the One Game Pledge, signed by cricketers across the country from schoolchildren to international stars.

- The pledge aims to ensure that the unique and inclusive nature of cricket in England and Wales is celebrated, respected and nurtured.

- It also gives us the opportunity to commit to a shared set of values that allow the game to develop and embrace the whole community, regardless of age, race, ability or gender.

- By signing the One Game Pledge you are signalling publicly that you welcome all newcomers to the game and share the passion and pride of those already involved.

The South African and Bangladeshi teams shake hands at the end of a Test match.

DISABILITY CRICKET

In recent years cricket has taken great strides towards
becoming a fully inclusive sport. England now has
international teams for deaf people and blind people,
and there are a growing number of domestic teams for
people with physical and mental disabilities. There are now
more opportunities than ever before for cricketers with
disabilities across a number of different forms of the game.

FORMATS

Where possible, disability cricket is
played in accordance with the MCC
laws of cricket. A few amendments
have been made to cater for
impairments and disabilities.

Blind cricket
In blind cricket the players are
categorised according to the level
of sight loss. The ball is made of
moulded plastic with steel ball
bearings inside to make it rattle.

Deaf cricket
To play the international game,
all cricketers with a hearing
impairment must have a hearing
loss of 55 decibels or less in their
better ear. Digital hearing aids
must be removed when they
take the field.

Learning disability cricket
International Learning Disability
Sport is overseen by the world
governing body INAS-FID, the
International Sports Federation
for People with an Intellectual
Disability. INAS rules state that
to play sport as an athlete with
a learning disability, you must
have an IQ of 75 or less.

Disabled players in action in the
Disability Cricket Regional finals.

PHYSICAL DISABILITY CRICKET

Currently there is no recognised international cricket for people with physical disabilities. One of the barriers that needs to be overcome is standardising a classification system that will be accepted globally. It is important to make sure that players in disability cricket are matched against others with similar disabilities.

The UK domestic structure has adopted the DSE (Disability Sports Events) profiling system, otherwise known as the Coaches Guide to Functional Ability, for athletes with physical impairments. The system is currently being reviewed to help disability cricket move forward and keep providing the best opportunities for those wanting to play the game.

For general information on disability cricket visit www.ecb.co.uk/ development/disability-cricket/ For more information on learning disability cricket see www.inas-fid.org/index.html

Some disabled players enjoy a day at the Oval cricket ground.

INDEX

- *to gain attention, where people seek the company of others so that they might be the centre of attention.*

The purported importance of affiliation and affiliative behaviour is supported by Hogg and Vaughan (1995) who say, 'the need to affiliate underlies the way in which we form interpersonal relationships'. They point out that early social psychological writers such as McDougall (1908) tried to explain affiliative behaviour in terms of instinct (for example, humans are born with a sociable, gregarious nature); he thus linked humans to other animals who live in colonies or herds. This explanation fell out of favour with the establishment of behaviourism. Watson (1913) contested that 'simply accounting for a behaviour like herding by calling it a herding instinct is no explanation at all' (Hogg and Vaughan, 1995). Contemporary accounts tend to focus upon affiliation as a human need and motivation and the consequences of enforced deprivation of opportunities for affiliation. Much of the empirical research has focused upon affiliation and the development of sociability and attachments in young children (e.g. Trevarthen (1980) showed that infants as young as two months of age demonstrated a desire to interact with their mothers, even via closed-circuit television transmission but not pre-recorded replays!) and non-human animals (e.g. the famous series of studies carried out by Harlow and Harlow, 1959–1962 on the effects of maternal deprivation on infant monkeys). Bowlby (e.g. 1969) also studied affiliative behaviours in infants, showing that infants use many 'strategies', such as crying and smiling, to maintain proximity with their caregiver. He argued that denial of affiliative 'access' can lead to the failure to develop warm and secure attachment bonds. Hogg and Vaughan (1995) say, 'For Bowlby, attachment behaviour is not limited to the mother/infant experience, but can be observed throughout the life-span, especially in emergencies'. They quote a study by Feeney and Noller (1990) which showed that different attachment styles in childhood, such as secure, avoidant and anxious, could be picked up in the way their romantic relationships were formed in adult life.

However, it is not just any old person we want to affiliate with. Schachter (1959) showed that at times of stress and uncertainty we prefer to be in the company of others rather than alone and furthermore prefer the company of others in a similar position (at least this was true for the American college females in his study). It could also be argued that the people we most seek affiliation with are those we like and love, which (rather tortuously) brings us to attraction.

Attraction

Much of the psychological research into social and interpersonal relationships has been carried out in North America and reflects the importance of 'partnership' relationships (particularly romantic love, couples and marriage/co-habitation). As Moghaddam et al. (1993) have pointed out, this has led to an emphasis upon research into relationships which are individualistic, voluntary and temporary, as opposed to those characteristic of non-Western cultures which tend to be collective, obligatory and permanent (see Humphreys, 1966, for discussion). With this focus upon the romantic couple it is perhaps unsurprising that a good deal of research has focused upon attraction and the initial stages of relationship formation. However, this does leave the research open to accusations of ethnocentricity and there being almost a whole world of 'taken-for-granteds' (e.g. romantic love; heterosexuality) and 'under-studied' relationships. We shall return to these concerns in Revisions and reconceptualisations.

Few of us who live in the Western world have not been aware – at least at some point in our lives – of the emphasis our cultures place upon physical beauty and 'looking good' (for example, as illustrated by the prevalence of eating disorders such as anorexia nervosa in these current historical times when thin is beautiful). Therefore our first port of call is physical attractiveness.

PHYSICAL ATTRACTIVENESS

Several studies (e.g. Dion, 1972; Sigall and Ostrove, 1975; Cash et al., 1977; Dipboye et al., 1977) have shown that 'attractive' people (even 'attractive' children in the case of the Dion study) consistently receive more favourable judgements from people. These include lighter recommended sentences in a trial, greater likelihood of success in job interviews and more estimates of psychological well-being and adjustment.

A study was carried out by Landy and Sigall (1974) in which male students were asked to grade two essays which differed in quality. The good and poor essays were each paired with photographs of the supposed writer, in one instance an attractive and in the other a 'relatively unattractive' female. As Hogg and Vaughan (1995) observe, 'Sad to relate, better grades were given to the attractive female'. These writers also cite a study by Cunningham (1986) which would seem to show that 'American males found women with "cute" faces more attractive', and defined 'cute' as being a function of childlike appearance (' "childlike" appearance in women might signal youth and hence greater childbearing potential').

We might well anticipate that many women (and men too!) would question the ethical soundness of such sexist studies which cast women as objects for judgement by men. One could seriously question not only the sexism of the male respondents but also of the studies themselves. Perhaps more worryingly, such studies may be seen as 'justifying' a natural order of things in which men and women are cast into such roles.

Not only has the 'supporting-sexism' aspect of much of the research in this field been questioned by many critics, but the contrived methodology of many other studies has been seen as problematic. The following two are classic examples.

In 1966, Walster et al. carried out what has come to be known in many circles as the 'computer dance' study. 'Fresher' students (752 in all) at the University of Minnesota were asked to fill in a questionnaire and were then given tickets for a dance having been informed that a computer had been used to analyse the data and make ideal matches; in fact, couples (all male/female, of course) were allocated to each other at random. The students were judged (without their knowledge or consent) for physical attractiveness.

> *Physical attractiveness proved to be the single most important factor that determined liking, for both males and females, and the single best predictor of how likely it was that a woman would be asked out again – regardless of the man's.*

> (Gross, 1996)

This was interpreted as showing that the men were aiming to maximise their 'gain' by dating the most attractive women, irrespective of their own physical attractiveness. However, criticisms were made that the study lacked ecological validity because the partners had been pre-chosen, and in Western cultures this is not usual practice. Consequently, in 1969 Walster and Walster carried out another computer dance study, but this time the students were able to meet each other beforehand and were able to state what kind of partner they would like (in terms of physical attractiveness), and this time it emerged that they sought comparability with their own attractiveness rather than simply judging the most attractive as most desirable for them.

This later finding has been interpreted as either supporting the so-called *matching hypothesis* (we seek relationships with those of similar 'status' to ourselves) or that we do not endeavour to form relationships with those more attractive than ourselves because of a fear of rejection (Huston, 1973).

A further exploration of the matching hypothesis was made by Murstein (1973) in which photographs of 'engaged or steady' couples were taken and compared with 'random' couples (i.e. two people who did not know each other and were photographed together only for the purpose of the experiment). Judgements of the attractiveness of all the people in the photographs were made, and it was found that, compared to the control ('random couples') condition, the real pairs received very similar judgements. Murstein concluded:

> *Individuals with equal market value for physical attractiveness are more likely to associate in an intimate relationship such as premarital engagement than individuals with disparate values.*

Note the use of the phrase 'market value'; this notion, which is emphasised by exchange theories or relationships (see Humphreys, 1996, for a review), views relationship 'activity' as any other form of economic activity, in which costs and benefits are weighed in the process of buying and selling. We need hardly point out that models using such analogies are hardly appropriate to cultures which are not characterised by economic systems and ways of life which are non-capitalist.

SIMILARITY

Clore and Byrne (1974) have formulated a 'law of attraction' which states that there is a linear relationship between the attraction people feel for others and the similarity of their attitudes. In terms of folk wisdom, this would support the saying 'birds of a feather flock together' rather than 'opposites attract'. And there is considerable empirical support for this contention.

Two classic studies in this area were carried out by Theodore Newcombe (1943, 1961). In the first of the studies, Newcombe found that female students at a particular university college in USA (Bennington College), noted at the time for the 'liberal' attitudes held by staff and students, adapted their own attitudes – even if they were previously conservative – in order to be more similar to others and be liked by their peers. In the later study, students were given rent-free accommodation for which they had to fill in numerous questionnaires at regular intervals. The questionnaires measured their attitudes and values. It was found that, in the first few weeks, attraction was most associated with *proximity* (a factor established earlier in a study by Festinger et al. (1950) which showed that, in a housing complex which was studied, people chose those who lived closest to them as their friends).

Newcombe's 1961 study showed, however, that as the semester progressed, proximity became a less powerful determinant of attraction and liking and was replaced by attitudinal similarity. Why should this be the case? Rubin (1973 cited in Gross, 1996) argues that the following five factors may go some way to explaining the phenomenon:

- Agreement may provide a basis for engaging in joint activities.
- A person who agrees with us helps to increase our confidence in our own opinions which enhances our own self-esteem.
- Most people are vain enough to believe that anyone who shares their own views must be a wise and wonderful person.
- Communication may be easier for people who agree about matters which are important to them.
- We may believe that people who hold similar views to ourselves will like us and so, it is argued, we will then like them (this process, which has been extensively researched in its own right, is called *reciprocal liking*).

For once there is even cross-cultural evidence to support the thrust of argument here. Brewer (1968) studied 30 different tribal groups in East Africa and carried out 1,500 interviews. She found that three factors were associated with liking others. In order of importance these were:

- perceived similarity;
- actual distance between the tribal groups;
- perceived educational and economic 'advancement'.

COMPLEMENTARITY

Is it always the case, then, that we like people who we perceive to be similar to ourselves? According to Winch (1958), who proposed a complementary-needs hypothesis, the answer is no – we are attracted to opposites. He interviewed married couples and argued that, in terms of their needs from the relationship and from the other person, there are two forms of complementary needs: nurturant-receptive and dominant-submissive. However, it has been pointed out that 'often a partner will be nurturant in one situation and receptive in another, or dominant in some areas but not in others', and Winch's views have not been well corroborated empirically (Hayes, 1994).

Notice how we have slipped into a cosy niche. By 'getting our heads down' and scanning through psychological models of liking and attraction between couples and friends (many of them short term in nature, most of them concerned with the initial aspects of relationships, almost all of them carried out in North America or Western Europe), we are guilty of ignoring or being blind to many 'taken-for-granteds'. We are assuming that we are relatively free agents to make and break relationships and that human relationships are essentially universal. Do 'factors' such as race and sexuality, for example, have no influence? How well do our standard psychological tools and processes (such as the questionnaire and the laboratory experiment) 'get to grips' with the profundity of human social relationships? Let's start challenging!

Revisions and reconceptualisations

Let us begin by identifying two critical perspectives on the psychology of relationships: a cross-cultural one and one reflecting postmodernism.

Ethnocentricity

Moghaddam et al. (1993) argue that much of what is researched and reported in Western psychology is simply not applicable to the majority of non-Western cultures. They say social relationships in Western cultures tend to be *individualistic, voluntary* and *temporary* whereas those in non-Western societies are more frequently *collectivist, involuntary* and *permanent*. For example, family life in Britain tends to focus around a romantic pair and a (non-extended) nuclear family unit, and there is ever greater acceptance for co-habitation rather than marriage. In many non-Western societies, marriages are arranged, and kin and family ties are vastly more influential than in Britain. They make the case for psychological ethnocentrism when they say:

> *The cultural differences in interpersonal relationships reminds us that scientists, like everyone else, are socialised within a given culture. As*

a result, their theories and research are inevitably affected by this cultural experience. The cultural values and environmental conditions in North America have led North American social psychologists to be primarily concerned with first-time acquaintances, friendships and intimate relationships, primarily because these appear to be the relationships most relevant to the North American urban cultural experience.

(Moghaddam et al., 1993)

Postmodern perspectives

Postmodern thinking contributed to a further critique of traditional approaches to human relationships. Wood and Duck (1995) suggest a number of areas of reconceptualisations, some of which we discuss below in turn.

SITUATED ACCOUNTS, NOT LAWS; PERSPECTIVES NOT TRUTH

One of the most challenging ideas of postmodern thinking to traditional psychology is that our theories, views or discourses are always 'positioned' in a historical, cultural and personal context (see also Chapter 3). In other words, there could be many different theories explaining the same phenomena from different points of view. While such theories will differ, they will be equally 'true', shedding light on how the world (or relationships, in our case) looks from that particular point of view. Since most academics in the West have been middle class, male, white and heterosexual, dominant perspectives in the study of relationships reflect the values and life experiences specific to this group. Thus, as Wood and Duck (1995) point out, mainstream psychology has tended to focus on instrumental and exchange perspectives, while 'more usually feminine affiliative perspectives, and the study of communal orientations, processes, needs and mutuality' have been neglected. For example, Argyle (1994) proposes a number of 'human needs' which, he argues, are satisfied in personal relationships. The idea is that we 'get something out of relationships'. This very notion sits rather uncomfortably in relation to the findings of researchers and theorists whose work has been more 'woman centred'. For example, both Carol Gilligan (1982) and Nancy Chodorow (1987) argue that women are socialised to relate to others in ways which are more closely associated with 'giving' and 'nurturing' behaviours rather than with focusing on their own needs and thus 'taking'. Moreover, among other 'human needs' cited by Argyle are the following: 'dominance', 'sex' and 'aggression'. These particular three characteristics are typically associated with cultural constructions of masculinity. Research on same-sex friendships has long since documented that male friendships involve displays of 'dominance' and 'aggression', and in intimate relationships it is men who most often report a 'sex' interest, whereas women appear more concerned with 'love' (Peplau and Gordon, 1985). To call such characteristics 'human' is to ignore the fact that, in essence, we are talking about male concerns. In fact, relationship research, like other research in psychology which talks about 'human' nature, has often ended up obscuring female points of view and interests. It thus involves an androcentric bias (i.e. a male point of view).

However, there are many other, not just women's, points of view which have also been excluded from the study of relationships in psychology. Wood and Duck (1995) point out that we know very little about relationships between lesbian, gay, disabled, working-class, black and other people who belong to more marginalised groups in society. Researching such relationships has two main implications. In the first instance, such studies show us that whatever we have considered to be 'normal' in terms of, say, characteristics of same-sex friendships, attraction or love relationships are in fact specific to the middle-class, Western, white population. The second implication of such studies is that, by listening to the perspectives of 'others' or by allowing their 'voices' expression, issues around the notion of empowerment and greater democratisation of the discipline are addressed.

Let's take an example. In mainstream research on friendship, gender is regarded as a central variable. In other words, it is not class, education, 'race', age, marital status, sexuality, neighbourhood, particular work environment, etc. that are considered as factors shaping the 'type' of friendship people have with members of their own sex. While such variables are often not sufficiently attended to, from this kind of research we have accumulated 'evidence' that male and female same-sex friendships typically differ along a number of dimensions. Male friendships tend to stress competition; a certain degree of personal autonomy; doing things (rather than disclosing and discussing personal issues); interacting, often in groups (rather than in dyads) on the basis of clearly established rules (Bakan, 1966; Wright, 1982). On the other hand, female friendships tend to be more cooperative; inclined towards making and sustaining connections with others through 'disclosing' or talking; and doing so more often in dyads (rather than groups) (Gilligan, 1982; Miller, 1986).

However, more recent studies have begun to question the notion that 'types' of friendships can be attributed so easily to the sex of persons involved. A study by Franklin II (1992) can be used to illustrate this point. In it, the researcher takes into account the sex, but also the social class and 'race' of the individuals involved. Franklin II found that black, working-class men share 'warm, holistic, nurturant and intimate' same-sex friendships. On the other hand, 'upwardly mobile' or middle-class black men have friendships which are 'cool, non-intimate and segmented'. Such studies suggest that it is not sex *per se* which shapes the apparent characteristics of friendship. Franklin II directs the attention to the specific conditions in which black, working-class men develop their sense of identity. For many, self-reliance, economic success, political power and family provision (i.e. socially endorsed male values) are frustrated by institutional and other forms of racism. The emphasis on commitment to their same-sex friendships serves as a buffer against a hostile society. Black men who move up the social ladder and thus gain a further entry into a social world of white, male culture appear to develop friendships more like white men's, i.e. based on competition, autonomy and separation. What such studies illustrate is that many psychological theories have developed typologies based on the experiences of white people and have ignored sociopolitical contexts which can account for apparent differences between women's friendships and men's friendships. In addition, such studies allow for the celebration (rather than condemnation) of friendships outside apparent established (white) norms. Appreciating the political dimension of working-class, black men's friendships has led some researchers to consider ways in which the internalisation of other than mainstream (white men's) sociopolitical ideology can lead to a situation where black men can form productive, warm and intimate relationships (Madhubuti, 1990).

Language as representational

Mainstream psychology treats language as representational, i.e. it assumes that 'behind' concepts used in the discipline there resides some 'object-like, real' thing. Postmodernism has challenged this by arguing that the very concepts we employ are then given a form of reality by what people do. Language, then, does not simply reflect reality but constructs it. From this point of view, when psychologists were studying areas such as 'attraction', they were not simply 'discovering' how attraction functions and whom people were finding attractive; rather they were involved in a constructive 'reality-making' activity already going on in the culture. For example, the notion that beautiful women and strong men attract and then couple is familiar to all people in Western culture, from their exposure to the first fairy story to the latest romantic film they saw. For postmodernists, this formula constitutes 'attraction', and it is a culturally constructed myth. Psychology has reproduced it. In its findings, it has 'discovered' that typically men look for beauty in women and women for status in men (e.g. Feingold, 1992). Thus, psychology, by stating what has already been said but with a voice which carries a certain authority of 'science', has joined all the other voices in the culture saying the same thing. With them, it has contributed towards the construction of 'attraction' as naturally occurring phenomena (typically) between heterosexuals and towards the construction of 'attractiveness' as a static quality belonging to the individual. Postmodern and critical thinkers in other disciplines (with which psychology tends not to engage) have long since questioned such an assumption. Typically the questions asked are:

- How is the concept of attraction socially constructed?
- In what social practices is the construct embedded so that we come to believe in it and be affected by it in our lives?
- What are the implications of these kinds of constructions for the continuing inequalities between the sexes?

Figure 5.2 The matching of beauty in women with status in men is a widely accepted formula in Western society

To answer such questions, critical thinkers tend to expand their focus of investigation and to examine larger cultural context. For example, Tseëlon (1995) makes the following statement with regard to the work of critical theorists such as Giddens (1991) and Harré (1991):

. . . within a cultural framework of late Capitalism, in a consumer culture obsessed with appearance, the status of the body has been transformed from a fixed, natural given to a malleable, cultural product. Regimes of dietary management, building and maintenance, as well as complete reshaping and sculpting of the body are associated with its conception as an instrument of pleasure, and self expression. The preservation of the body-beautiful, body-young and body-healthy indicate on the one hand a desire to control nature by defying mortality, and on the other hand the fashioning of personal identity.

The very emphasis on attractiveness, then, according to such theorists, is not something 'natural' but rather it is borne out of 'late Capitalism' in which available technology offers possibilities to reshape the body. Capitalism also tends to treat the body as an object for consumption with a value attached to it, which in turn affects one's sense of personal identity. While 'fashioning personal identity' is important for both sexes, it is especially so for women. Reading mainstream psychology, one can gain the impression that women 'have' beauty and men are 'attracted' to it. Critical theorists have challenged the notion that 'beauty' is somehow a 'natural' feminine preoccupation by directing the attention to social practices which produce and maintain this idea. Film, photography, television, entertainment, adverts, women's magazines, pornography, pin-ups, paintings, posters – everywhere one goes in Western cultures, there are images of beautiful and perfect women. Mainstream women's magazines continually instruct women on how to take care of their skin, hair, lips, hips, bottoms, breasts, legs, hands, nails, body hair, size, fitness, dress and so on. In fact, many women's magazines are more like manuals on female appearance. There are, of course, vested interests in the promotion of the notion that women are 'naturally' interested in beauty. Millions are made each year by (mostly men) working in fashion, perfume, make-up, dieting and other industries. Seid (1988), for example, cites the following figures associated with 'beauty' industries in the United States: $32 billion thinness industry and £20 billion youth industry.

Given this cultural context in which women are continually reflected back to themselves in terms of appearance, it is not surprising that most women will be concerned with the way they look. Moreover, 'looks' continue to influence life opportunities for women. There are social pressures which can influence where a woman finds a job and how much she earns. Naomi Wolf (1990) refers to this as the PBQ factor: Professional Beauty Qualification. In other words, the desire to be beautiful can be seen not as rooted in some deep, 'feminine nature' but rather within the context of a social world which discriminates against people on the basis of sex and female appearance in particular.

The social construction of 'beauty' as a female concern can also be investigated in terms of more micro social interactions. In *Cults in America: programme for paradise*, Willa Appel (1983) presents some examples of the ways in which beauty consultants are trained to evoke in their clients insecurities and fears which will then make them buy beauty products. Thus consultants are trained to move really close to the faces of the potential customers, to stare fixedly into their eyes, to say things such as, 'You use *what* on your face?', 'Well, if you are happy with those little pimples', 'You are destroying the delicate skin under your eyes', 'If you don't stop doing what you're doing on your face, in ten years your whole face will be a mass of creases' (cited in Wolf, 1990). Such examples demonstrate the conscious effort made by those interested in making profit from 'female attractiveness' to persuade women to believe in the 'beauty myth'.

That there are cultural pressures on women to spend more money from their income (than men do) on appearance (so that mostly men ultimately make more money) is unfair (Wolf, 1990). However, there is also another way in which notions of female 'beauty' are implicated in practices of inequality between the sexes. John Berger (1972) analysed Western paintings and demonstrated how traditionally women's bodies have been represented in such a way as to appeal to a male observer. Since then, many others have observed that, in Western culture, it is women who are typically displayed, looked at and surveyed in terms of their bodily characteristics; women are the spectacle and men the spectator (Tseëlon, 1995). This preoccupation in the work of critical writers ties up with the notion that the 'gaze' is an intrusive exercise of power. Coward (1984) says:

> *Men defend their scrutiny of women in terms of the aesthetic appeal of women. But this so-called aesthetic appreciation of women is nothing less than a decided preference for a 'distanced' view of the female body. The aesthetic appeal of women disguises a preference for* looking *at women's bodies, for keeping women separate, at a distance, and the ability to do this.*

The implied power dynamics between the typical male looker and the female object are absent from traditional work on attraction in psychology. In this way, for critics, psychological theories on attraction have served to naturalise and legitimise a male right of 'looking at' women. Critical writers have shown how women do not have 'natural beauty' any more than men do (if women did have it, why continually instruct them on how to be beautiful and why spend millions on manufacturing female 'beauty'?). In the same way, men are not 'natural lookers'. The notion that 'a man can't help looking' at women represents an undeserved, socially constructed, male entitlement to women's bodies in a male-dominated culture. While at times it is argued that men like women so much they can't help looking at them, the flip side of this 'right to look' positions men also to make derogatory comments regarding women's appearances, to sexually harass women, to exploit women in pornography, and at times to refuse them work. For critical researchers, the issue of attraction is not something which goes on 'innocently' and 'naturally' between members of the opposite sex; rather it is a socially constructed phenomenon deeply embedded in the power structure of the culture.

Profound contextuality

Mainstream psychological research tends to assume that one can 'pick' an 'object' out of the social domain and investigate it objectively in terms of its own specific properties. In the area of human relationships, such objects have been attraction, affiliation, friendship, love relationships, the family, etc. In the section above, we argued that 'attraction', for example, is not a naturally occurring phenomenon. Another way of investigating this topic is to treat it as an 'object' of discourse which is embedded in and maintained by a variety of modern social practices.

In general, postmodern scholarly work tends to be more complex, paying attention to specific details of the researched topic and to its multiple layers of embeddedness in the social fabric. To illustrate the notion of 'profound contextuality' of a particular topic, we shall take as an example a research paper on the 'family' by Holstein and Gubrium (1994). Just like the concept of 'attraction', mainstream psychology has tended to treat the 'family' as if behind the label there resides something real and solid – an object-like entity. By contrast, Holstein and Gubrium direct our attention to how we can see the 'family' as if it is something which is unstable, undefinable and more fluid. Its various aspects are shared by members of our culture and also alter from one situation to another and from one speaker to another. The authors also point out that the notion of the 'family' as we know it is a modern invention and did not exist prior to the early modern period (Nicholson, 1988). Today, however, the private group of parents and children is what we understand as family. Moreover discourses of the family tell a story about family responsibilities, about the necessity to sustain long-lasting ties, to be caring and sharing, to live together, to have custodial rights, to share living accommodation. Such features of what we call the 'family' are sustained in social practices (e.g. for the law) and also in the very ways we talk to one another about it. Take, for example, the following exchange between a father and his son cited by Holstein and Gubrium (1990). The father accuses the son of failing in his filial role:

> *You don't keep in touch. You won't even talk on the phone. Or even when you do, you are just plain disagreeable . . . You don't care*

about your mother's feelings, you don't even feel for her at all. Do you realise what she goes through worrying about you? You know, you don't give us a damn thing. You could be a stranger. No consideration. No warmth. Nothing. You only act like a son when you need us. Where's your family loyalty, anyway?

The discourse of the family dictates that a son ought to keep in touch, he ought to be considerate, warm, loyal. In his response, the son does not challenge in any way such (socially constructed) 'features' of the family; these are shared. Rather he tries to establish ways in which he is actually a 'son':

Come on. You know that I care. It's just hard for me. I come by, but I just don't want to start worrying you, so I don't say too much . . . I thought I was doing something good for you by trying to stay out of your hair . . . I get pretty screwed up sometimes, so I try to stay away when I might have a bad day. I know what it does to Mom, and I don't want to do that to her. I don't want to hurt her . . . I got my problems and I know they get to you, but you're all the family I have.

This exchange represents an example of how, in social interaction, the 'family' is continually constructed and reconstructed as a meaningful entity. The son offers an account of his behaviour aiming to illustrate that he did what he did because he 'cared'. It seems he was driven to behave in ways which appeared not like those of a 'son' only because he was a better 'son' still.

The above exchange also illustrates how discourse about the family can be used functionally, i.e. to accuse someone else and to justify oneself. Similar 'functions' of the discourse can be observed in many different locations – between family members, in court procedures, in conversations with friends, in political debates, in therapies of various kinds. Moreover, in such different locations, despite the fact that the same term (i.e. 'the family') is deployed, it is not always imbued with the same meanings. Thus the meaning of what is actually a 'family' varies from one place to another. In particular, Holstein and Gubrium direct the attention to two competing definitions of the term in modern times. Both of these, the authors argue, are institutionally embedded. They present examples of two family therapy agencies. In the first, 'A functional family is one in which parents or other properly responsible adults are in control, making the consequential decisions in the home'. Typically, the aim of the therapy is to establish traditional authority, preferably of the father, in the cases in which it has been eroded. The second type of family therapy 'orients the domestic order as a democracy . . . where everyone's feelings are equally important'. The aim of the therapy here is to establish effective mutual communications between equal members of the household. When these two models are put into practice, other differences emerge. Family members are expected to speak in different ways and to have different physical composure. For example, the actual seating arrangements would be such that in the 'traditional' family, the father would typically take the 'power seat', an action which would be considered inappropriate in the 'democratic' one. What is 'functional' and 'healthy' in one institutional setting, is seen as dysfunctional and unhealthy in the other.

Different constructions of the family may emerge in certain social situations. Holstein and Gubrium present an example of an exchange between a community mental-health psychiatrist and a judge. While the former sees the family as a group of people who provide a 'supportive environment', the judge is concerned with 'controlling'. In this way, Holstein and Gubrium argue, 'family' constructs support the organisational outlooks and interests of the various parties involved. Overall, Holstein and Gubrium conclude that: 'Embeddedness, then, is "layered", various interpretative domains and concerns overlapping to provide diverse ways of constructing the family meaning'.

Decentred selves

In Chapter 3, we argued that while mainstream psychology treats the individual as a coherent entity, postmodern psychologists have proposed that subjectivity is multiple, contradictory and inconsistent. In a similar way, postmodern notions have challenged traditional views on human relationships. Mainstream psychology has tended to turn a blind eye to contradictions, conflict and inconsistencies in relationships, preferring to look at 'satisfaction' and 'harmony' (Wood and Duck, 1995).

However, for psychologists drawing on the postmodern perspective, our relationships are embraced by dominant discourses which are themselves contradictory. Wendy Hollway (1989), for instance, investigated heterosexual love relations. She identified three main cultural discourses and argued that discourses are 'gendered', i.e. that each discourse tells how one ought to behave on the basis of one's sex. For example, one of the three discourses she identified is the so-called *male sexual drive* discourse. On the basis of this discourse, modern Western society assumes that it is men who, somehow by nature, have greater sexual appetite and are more sexually active than women. The man who wolf-whistles at a passing woman in the street enters, to use the appropriate terminology here, as a 'subject' in the 'male sexual drive' discourse and places the woman as an 'object' to his own desire. Acting out what is called here one's 'subject position in discourse' (i.e. if you are male and act out what the discourse says men do) gives the appearance of 'reality' to the claims made by the discourse in the first place. In other words, in this case a man might appear a more active sexual being than a woman, not because he is so by 'nature', but simply because there is a cultural discourse which is shared with others and which instructs him how to act on the basis of his sex.

The other two discourses which Hollway identifies are the so-called *to have/hold* discourse and the *permissive* discourse. The former, according to her, has its roots in Western Christian traditions on the basis of which monogamy, loyalty and commitment between individuals in a couple are emphasised. This discourse is gendered too, since it is the man who is placed in one specific position – namely, that of the head of the family – and the woman in another – that of the home-maker. According to the 'have/hold' discourse, sex is represented as something which ought to be done in a 'committed' relationship; the 'permissive' discourse, on the other hand, which originated more recently in the 1960s and the 'hippy era', suggests otherwise. While on the basis of this last discourse, women are also seen to be sexually active, according to Hollway, male sexuality still remains to be represented as if more active. The reason for this continuous 'gendering' of subjects is to do with another important feature of discourse, that discourses are not pure and thus meanings from other discourses (in this case the 'male sexual drive' discourse) spill over to permeate meanings of even apparently oppositional discourses (such as the 'permissive' one).

Since all three discourses are circulated in our culture at present, Hollway argues that, to a greater or lesser extent, people will move between them and experience their contradictions as if located in themselves or in the relationship. Thus, for example, a man can be a subject in both the 'male sex drive' discourse and the 'have/hold' one. While the former tells him that he ought to be interested in every passing woman, the other speaks about monogamy and faithfulness. There are also, of course, various institutional settings which are themselves more or less located in one or another of these discourses. For example, Fine and Addelston (1996) and Messner (1992) all present accounts of the ways in which, in male-dominated institutional environments (law schools in the former and sports organisations in the latter), a culture evolves in which the 'male sex drive' discourse flourishes. Messner, for example, cites one young male athlete positioning himself in 'male sex drive' discourse thus:

> *But you* gotta *be involved to the point where you get them into bed, you know, and* fuck *'em, or something like that, yeah, that's real important (laughs); but as far as being intimate or close, I wasn't. And that wasn't really important. Just so I could prove my heterosexuality, it was real important. But I always wanted to look good to females, 'cause I didn't have the personality (laughs) to get them into bed! So I wanted to have the body and the, uh, the sort of friends around who, uh, who admired me in some sort of way, to have that pull.*

Messner argues that in this specific context, the 'male sex drive' discourse functions to cement friendships between male athletes (particularly since, in other ways, they are competitive and antagonistic towards one another) and secondly, it functions to alleviate fears of intimacy with women. However, this does not mean that men enter the discourse unproblematically or stay in it as subjects all the time. Some (like the participant cited below) experience conflict once they enter a love relationship and thus also become subjects in the 'have/hold' discourse. So, Frank, a basketball and tennis player says: